Good Kittens, Good Cats

Good Kittens,

*Poems and Stories
of Joy, Humor
and Loss*

Good Cats

Wayne W. Lysobey

*I dedicate this book to all the cats
I know, have known, and will know.*

Contents

Cat Haiku

Oh furry felines
Purring so contentedly
I envy you so

Cat Haiku 2

Oh furry felines
Marvelous masters of life
Purring perfection

Leyden Jar Cats

Feline Owners to you I should mention

Cats are Leyden Jars of affection

You scratch behind ears

Be it days be it years

Then you get back all of the attention

Prince Among Cats

He must have been able to hear the step van from half a mile away.

Hobart was a big gray striped tabby. A prince among kitties. We had a second floor apartment. Hobart could climb a tree and come in through our bedroom window. The mousing was pretty good around the old grounds, and Hobart would frequently bring us presents. Usually this was in the middle of the night.

"Wrow erwow" we would hear. It was difficult for Hobart to speak clearly with his mouth full of mouse. We developed a mouse removal routine. A wide mouth mason jar and an index card worked well together. Hobart usually held on to the mouse until I was ready with the jar.

Hobart would drop the mouse. I would quickly cover it with the mouse jar. I kept this jar next to the bed. It was labeled "mouse jar", just in case we forgot what it was for.

"Good boy" Bev and I would exclaim. I would slide the index under the jar and flip the jar right side up. Outside to the yard I would go and let the mouse go. Wonder if it was ever the same mouse.

My Chevy Step Van was a work vehicle. Like a bread delivery van or smaller UPS truck. I think it had its own noise signature. I would park in the lower side parking lot. There were some old stonework walls and steps going up to the side of the house. There were about seven apartments there.

Hobart and I had a routine. By the time I had pulled in and parked, Hobart was usually sauntering down the steps to meet me.

"It's the Hobartski Burger," I would say to him. His striped, gray tail would be held high. "OK, let's get the mail". He would follow me to the mailroom. I would pick up the mail, just a boy and his cat. We were relaxed hombres, but we knew what was coming. Out of the mailroom we would go, nonchalantly, turning to the right-

"OK, lets go!!!!!!!!!" I would start to sprint. Hobart would be right at my heels in his easy cat gallop. A miniature gray cheetah. A prince among cats, lord of his domain.

"Come on, I'm gonna beat ya!!" We would round the corner to the front porch. Me laughing like a little kid.

Always, always, always, he would wait for the turn and then, with a burst of cat speed he would be waiting on the top of the porch steps as if he had been there all along. I sometimes had some smiles and funny looks from people that happened to be on the porch at those times!

There Is A Little Kitten

There is a little kitten
With cute little paws
She likes to climb your pant leg
With sharp little claws

There is a little furry friend
Who likes to get her treats
If she doesn't get them
She'll be tripping up your feet

There is a little kitty cat
Who sometimes seems a fiend
If you meet our kitten Magpie
You will know just what I mean

Gabe

There once was a kitten named Gabe
With the toilet paper he played
He shredded and chewed
And when he was through
Thought I think too long have I stayed

Cats

There's kitties there's kittens there's cats
They roll and they stretch and they scratch
They are bundles of fur
They purr and they purr
What more can I say about that

Gabe 2

Now Gabe he sure knows how to purr
As he gets you to scratch and pet fur
He's really quite charming
And oh so disarming
As he stretches and lets out a "murrr"

Gabe Kitty

Gabe's a pretty nice cat
Really no doubt about that
He murrs and he purrs
And he warms up your lap

Orange Cat

He's furry

He's purry

He curls up on my lap

He's something quite special

Our big orange striped cat

Thunder Paws

He rumbles round the second floor
He thunders down the stairs
His step is not too dainty
We call him Thunder Paws

He jumps onto our bed
In the early early morn
Get up get up come feed me
Demands our Thunder Paws

Just a lovable big orange kitty
Though perhaps he has some flaws
You'd know just what I mean
If you knew our Thunder Paws

Kitty Boy

Such a nice little kitty
With such sharps claws
With his furry little head
And furry little paws

When he sneaks up behind you
And stretches up real high
You may feel those claws stick in you
It can almost make you cry

He has no bad intentions
He is really quite a joy
Even though his claws might stick us
He is just our kitty boy

Archie

To Archie we've become quite attached

As he sits there and purrs on our laps

So warm and so furry

We forget all our worries

And all settle down for a nap

Trick Kitty

He stands on hind legs
He stands very tall
I call him trick kitty
He's loved by us all

Good Cat

You're a very good kitten good cat
But I just like to know where you're at
You hide and you play
Sometimes far away
So come when you're called that is that

Chubby Cat

Kitty kitty kitten
Kitty kitty cat
You're getting kinda chubby
Your getting kind a fat
I like to keep you happy
I like to feed you food
But when it comes to eating
You're always in the mood

Good Kitties Good Cats

Good kitties good kittens
Good kittens good cats
Vinny's getting skinny
And Gabe's getting fat
Archie is athletic
Leaping like a gazelle
While Gabe's a bit clumsy
But purrs very well
Vinny's slowing down
But he sits proud and tall
A three kitty family
That we love one and all

George the Halloween Cat

Not sure why we called him George

Just seemed to fit

He was the Halloween cat

He padded up the driveway

Shiny black fur

Halloween evening

Cool and collected

Looking like we belonged to him

And made our castle his castle

Hobart pounced on him in the hallway-

And then proceeded to lick him up good

A good kitty bath for George

This happened frequently

After one month George disappeared

Too many baths perhaps

Next Halloween we kept our eyes out

For any shiny black cats

Padding up the driveway

But no George

Maybe this year

Wally

He was the terror of the neighborhood
He prowled both day and night
He'd be there lurking in the bushes
He was an omnipresent sight

Scowling right up onto the porch
And peering through glass doors
Your territory vanishing
While his grew more and more

Little Kitten

She is just a little kitten
She is just a little cat
She is just our little furry friend
And there is no denying that

When she wants attention
She rolls around the floor
Showing off her furry belly
Getting cuter more and more

She is just our little kitten
We have had her fifteen years
She is a purring little fur ball
And she brings us much good cheer

Snowboarding Cat

There once was a snowboarding cat
He liked his trails steep and not flat
His claw side it did catch
In a deep powder patch
And he lost one more life going splat

Vinny

There once was a cat name of Vinny

Who was more lovable than he was brainy

He's growl and he'd race

All over the place

Sometimes he seemed rather insaney

Skunk Back Vinny

With that patch of white fur
That runs down his back
While much of his fur
Is really quite black
From a certain angle
From a certain view
He looks like a skunk
Just minus the phew!

Calico Cat

A calico cat
Can be very demanding
Our cat we called Autumn
Could be quite commanding

She liked Johnny Cash
With his deep gravelly voice
We played him a lot
It was her favorite choice

Be it dog be it cat
Or her people too
She ruled the roost
Till the day she was through

Shrew

A vole a mole or a shrew

The cat dropped it into my shoe

I'm glad that I took

A moment to look

Before turning that thing into goo

A Sunday Morning Rain

Cat one and cat two
They sat there all too quiet
They did not know what to do

Staring out the window
They sat there and they plotted
They sat there and they schemed

If you are very very lucky
They will soon be napping quietly
Doing mischief in their dreams

Midnight Thumping

Thump thump thump thump
Like the Telltale Heart it did beat
Thump thump thump thump
Pleasant dreams interrupted
Into sleep this sound did creep
Thump thump thump thump
Like a midnight metronome
A sinister sound but soon we found
Was our cat's tail keeping that beat

Cat On a Porch

A cat on a porch on a rainy day
Just sittin' in a rocking chairs
Just passin' time away

No deep thoughts no big concerns
Are getting in his way
Just a cat in a rocking chair
Just passin' time away

The weather might get better
The weather might get worse

So while my cat is chillin' out
I thought I'd write some verse

Just sittin' at my keyboard
Just passin' time away

Roger Dodger

Our orange boy called Roger
Or sometimes Roger Dodger
Would lay on his back
With paws in the air
Right out in the lawn
With nary a care
Sometimes passersby
Would just stare and stare
At the coolest dude ever
When Roger was there

Maggie

She can still jump
But not so spry as she used to be
She can jump onto the chair
Onto the bench
And sit on the warm modem

She can still jump onto the toilet
Onto the cabinet
Onto the sink
And there cajole us
To turn the water on

She can still jump
Carefully
Though she may falter
And she may fall
And we watch
And we know
That the day comes
When we will take her to the Vet
One last time

Hobart and the Straw-Colored Light

Have you seen death singing
In the straw-colored light
—Patti Smith from "Death Singing"

I haven't told many people the full extent of this story. He was just a cat some people would surely think. And then there was the straw-colored light.

He was not just a cat to me. Not to us. I have written of him before, but not about the death, the grieving and the straw-colored light.

He was a big cat. A big gray stripped tabby. A big lovable empathic mouser of a cat.

We had a red rabbits foot tied to a piece of red yarn. It was Hobart's favorite cat toy. I kept it hung in the doorway by the kitchen table. Hobart would sit in the hall at dinner, waiting. I would swing the red rabbit's foot his way. He would bat it back, a base hit every time. Bev and I have such fond memories from those days. A loaf of bread, a jug of wine, and thou- and Hobart. Those were the days my friends.

Before kids and a little before our first house Bev and I were sitting on the apartment couch having an argument. Nothing too serious, but voices were raised. Hobart trots into the room; jumps right onto Bev's lap and puts his two front paws on her shoulders. He was eye to eye with her. He didn't need words to get his point across. Clearly, he disapproved! He stopped that argument in its tracks. Or his tracks I suppose. Bev and I looked at each other, argument over, and knew this was some special cat.

We bought our first house, about two miles from the apartment. I guess Hobart missed the old place. The first time he was gone for over a week. We thought he was a goner. We looked, called and asked all around our new neighborhood. No Hobart. On a hunch I drove over to the old place. "Hobarttttt…"

Yup, he comes sauntering, and I mean sauntering, swaggering, happy as a mouser, out of the bushes and hops into the car.

Bev cried when we came home. Hobart went to his old stomping grounds about ten times before he settled into the new place. It got like "Do you want to get him this time, or should I go?"

There came a day, as such days will always come, when Hobart was no more.

Bev was in the house. She saw me stop the car in the driveway and get out. She says she knew right then Hobart was dead. I went inside. We cried. We sobbed. We mourned.

I keened. I didn't know the word then, but like a pilgrim at the Wailing Wall I rocked back and forth in grief. I haven't grieved like that for most people.

I woke up in a dream that night. Or a vision. Or perhaps a deeper reality. I lie on my bed on my back. There was light. Straw colored light. Electric spark, lightning colored, Jacob's Ladder arcing light. It streaked around my torso like a sheath, a vest of straw-colored light. Was I dreaming. I lie there thinking that very thing. I have seen death singing in the straw-colored light.

In the straw-colored light
In light rapidly changing
On a life rapidly fading
Have you seen death singing
Have you seen death singing
Patti Smith-*Death Singing*

Burial of a Cat

We buried a cat the other day

Jenny, our sometimes therapy cat

How do they know when that purr is needed

And come to your comfort

And tend to your healing

And warm you to your heart

We buried Jenny the other day

Hole deep in the flower garden

White cardboard coffin lowered in

Ornamental grasses planted

We were her people

Her time is done

And she suffers no more

And she is mourned

Magpie

And is it our own mortality

We worry about

When we worry about Magpie

Our twenty-year-old kitten

Deaf waif

Not so well groomed

Shedding fur

Yet purring still

Demanding still

Living on our warmth

On our love

Reminding us

This is not forever

Bathroom Cabinet

I moved the stand-alone cabinet in the downstairs half bathroom. I put it back closer to the wall.

We didn't need it close to the toilet anymore. The wooden cabinet has some water damage on the top. The corner closest to the pedestal sink is bubbled and crazed or cracked. That is the corner that Magpie got wet so frequently.

I guess it won't get wet so often now. Now it will be a reminder. A reminder of when that geriatric furry feline friend Magpie would jump from the toilet to the cabinet to the sink, there to wait with that cajoling, endearing, enchanting and determined look. That look that said why haven't you turned the water on for me yet?

Well Magpie doesn't need the cabinet to jump up to the sink anymore. She is done with earthly concerns. I know I will be catching myself looking into the bathroom, by habit, expecting to see the world's oldest kitten looking back at me with a "what is taking you so long" look in her eyes.

She will be missed. Rest In Peace Magpie.